Looking for Kerouac

Looking for Kerouac

Poems by

Mark Saba

Cover design by Shay Culligan
Cover image by Ingmar on Unsplash
Author photo by Joan Saba

ISBN: 979-8-90146-812-8
Library of Congress Control Number: 2026935117

Kelsay Books
502 South 1040 East, A-119
American Fork, Utah 84003
Kelsaybooks.com

For our poets uncelebrated who record the pulse
of an unprecedented time

Acknowledgments

Thank you to the following publications, in which versions of these poems previously appeared:

Abandon Journal: "Time Travel"
Agape Review: "A Secular *Our Father,*" "A Secular *Hail Mary*"
Brownstone Poets Anthology: "The Land of Peace"
Dhara: A Paradise Worth Fighting For Anthology: "From the Corner of My Eye," "Back in Place," "High Tide"
Ephemera: "Conscious," "Fossil Flowers," "A New Autumn," "The Great Escape"
GAS: Poetry, Art, and Music: "Louis Rakes the Hedges," "Switching Glasses" (nominated for *Best of the Net*)
Goats Milk Magazine: "Old Shirts," "Tabula Rasa," "On Reading the Death Certificate"
Maine Public Radio, Poets from Here: "Morning Sheds Light"
New Generation Beats Anthologies: "Dunkin' Doughnuts," "What Peg Are You?"
Pittsburgh Quarterly: "I Could Live There"
The Poet: "That Moment"
Poetry for Ukraine Anthology: "The Day the Bombs Fell"
The Somerville Times: "Pause"
Stone Circle Review: "What Do You Need for a History?"

Contents

I. INTERSECTIONS

Sunday Café 15
Ear Pods 16
What Peg Are You? 17
Men in Hoodies 19
Dunkin' Doughnuts 20
Cues 22
Replacing the Window 24
Looking for Kerouac 25
Life Artist 26
Sketching People 27
Writing in Wartime 28
Conscious 29
The Day the Bombs Fell 30
The 9/11 Memorial 31
Congressional Cemetery 32
Gertrude Stein 33
The Land of Peace 34
A Secular *Our Father* 35
A Secular *Hail Mary* 36
Blue 37

II. PORTRAITS

When Your Spouse Speaks in Clichés 41
Switching Glasses 42
That Day 43
Love Prayer 44
The Things We Bought 45

Sleep Doctor 46
One Willow 48
A Name 49
Just Before My Father Died 50
On Reading the Death Certificate 51
Waiting Patiently in My Grandfather’s Sardinia 53
The Boy at the Window 55
I Went to Visit My Mother’s Grave 57
A Flock of Birds 58
Sling 59
Memories Don’t Have Feet 61
Our Secret 62
Back in Place 63
Miscarriage 64
The Tending Tree 65
Time Travel 66

III. PAUSE

Stranded 71
Galaxy Eyes 73
Pause 74
Under Water 75
High Tide 76
The Great Escape 77
Fossil Flowers 78
Morning Sheds Light 80
The Trees Lay Their Shadows 81
I’m Out of Business 82
A New Autumn 83

Storm 84
Louis Rakes the Hedges 85
I Could Live There 86

IV. MEDITATIONS

What Do You Need for a History? 89
Quitter 90
I Keep Being Reborn 92
That Moment 93
At Ten Years Old 94
I Did 95
The News 96
In These Times 97
Tabula Rasa 98
Old Shirts 99
Today I Write, Not Paint 100
I Am a Rock Band 101
Stepping Out 102
Waiting for a Poem to Arrive 103
Rolling 104
From the Corner of My Eye 105
I'd Forgotten 106
First the Berlin Wall 107
The Runway 108

I.
INTERSECTIONS

Sunday Café

Ten-thirty on a Sunday morning—
so much time left, so much gone
and everyone just sitting here drinking coffee.

Ten-thirty on an autumn weekend, the peninsular park
jettisoned from weekdays, filled with bipeds
now cycling, now speedwalking, running

in form-fitting fabric; an allotted recreation
spinning on its circular path.
Even the coffee drinkers look to grasp

the moment, heads locked in defiance,
confusion, denial. This ten-thirty
stays infinite as blood spills

on the other side of the planet,
oceans trade currents
and the sun inches toward

another dispensable noon.

Ear Pods

Ear pods, iPods, seat pods
at the airport lounge. By the bar,
TV addicts watching a game

they never play. A lone guy eating,
eating again; young woman scouting
her compact computer. A coterie of cleaners

vacuuming, picking up dishes, erasing
the transient. Wide windows offering
a blinding daylight, muffling the roar

of jet engines and deep conversation.
Destinations unknown, travelers
wearing multicolored glasses

park themselves in limbo
and watch, watch time fly by
in a future once real, now imagined

while never uttering a word.

What Peg Are You?

Do you stand dumbfounded
browsing the shelves of a warehouse grocery store
as you strain to read the fine print
to discover which version of a piquant salsa
was designed for you?

Do you load the truck at the dock
filling it with cardboard boxes
that house wrapped specimens
of what must be consumed?

Do you discard the wrappers
in a receptacle hidden under the sink?
Do you carry the bin out to the curb
and keep it safe from marauding wildlife?

Are you the one who trucks it away
and dumps it once again
in a concealed location
far from the glittering shops
that stay open all night?

Does the cracking plant feed your family
with a paycheck cut from petroleum plastics
that house your bottle of shampoo?
Do you design the label, enticing us
to wash away the natural oils of your hair?

What about the berries you pick
that get stuffed into stiff containers
so safe on their voyage
to another continent, another season?

What if you stopped to ask a question:
What peg am I in this madness?
How would it be if I removed it
and it all came tumbling down,

the way leaves and needles fall every autumn
and, after one year, leave no trace?

Men in Hoodies

Men in hoodies, backs turned
so we see silhouettes
not the plans they read

written by anonymous minds.
Hands buried in nails
they follow even lines of studs

broken by empty window frames.
Music fills the background, keeps them tied
to a fleeting sense of home. Blizzards

powder their work, and they sweep it
away. Rain fills mud gullies that flow
near the foundation. They will never live

in this house, but they will see it
on the backs of their eyes
as they go to sleep—a trade of perfection

always out of reach.

Dunkin' Doughnuts

The young man on crutches
gives up his place in line.
I hesitate to stand in one

or the other, wondering
about this self-selection process.
How will I know what I want?

To the left, a woman who may not
speak English presses the screen randomly
then looks around as if answers

will come flying in from afar.
Is it okay to ask for help?
To the right, a young woman in miniskirt

knows exactly what she wants.
She commands the screen as well as
every detail of her life.

Both finish, the immigrant looking
as if she's just committed a crime,
the young woman marching off

to the pickup station. My turn.
I search for a small black coffee
and breakfast sandwich, no cheese

while holding back the anxiety of this first
experience—I've never been here before
and not sure I'll ever be back.

Orders complete, we wait.
The man on crutches has left.
Held hostage by our stomachs

our destinies lie in the hands of the order
takers. To them we are all equal
and yes, they often make mistakes.

Cues

Here's to the French maiden
who slept with the Iroquois

To the Eastern European Jew
who slept with the Palestinian

To the mid-century American Black
who fell in love with a WASP

To the conquistador
who caught the eye of an Amazonian

To the cleric
who let his blood run free

To the Mandarin
in bed with a Uighur

To the wartime Czech
who submitted to a Nazi

To the newly appointed dean
and the starstruck student

To those hints of DNA
that reveal our beginnings

The first and the last of us
and all those in betweens

Who hinted at disbelief
and left offspring as cues

For an alternate history.

Replacing the Window

A man on the elevator ladder
six stories above the world
is not concerned with his footing.

The White man inside tapes a long crack
and steadies the glass against
the Black man's scraping.

The old caulking resists removal.
How he jams the corners, throws
his weight against the divide.

In time the bad window releases
falling gently into the White man's arms.
For a short time air moves quickly

between the two spaces. Lucky
it's a nice day out there.
It takes two to fit the new glass

before the Black man outside descends
to prepare for another raising.
He waits for the day he can fly.

Looking for Kerouac

On the road from Connecticut to Maine
a route I've known too well
my wayfinder takes me off guard.
There must be an accident.

Safely removed from the highway
I find myself in twists and turns
passing saltbox colonial homes
as well as those less kept

that once belonged to newer immigrants
the French and Irish possibly
or other itinerants who stopped by
looking for work, or life.

I am confused, don't know
where I'm going, too trusting
that my car will find its way
along peripheral streets like

those of my Pittsburgh youth.
A sign reads *Lowell*
but in blind acquiescence
my mind shifts attention

to a book I'd just read.
Only then does it occur to me
that the author is buried nearby
though I may never know where.

Maybe he wanted it that way.

Life Artist

Is what he called himself
even wrote it on his calling card.
No business name, or logo
of subservient affiliation.

No history, no religion.
Just an acquaintance I met
from another country, a smiling
tow-headed young guy

who wanted to stay in touch
as he grew a new life
in a beautiful foreign land.
I didn't know what he saw

in me, another transient
from the opposite coast.
Could it be that he offered
a hint, a recognition

that nothing is as it seems
that there against the blue
of San Francisco Bay
we could plumb our own depths

and arise as something new,
a defiance of the affectations
of upscale lifestyle?
I conceded, took his card

and lost it, never called.

Sketching People

The first lines faint, finding their places
as they skip over a white abyss, edges
deepening, highlights phantasms.

Form follows direction, dimensions
asserting themselves until a face appears,
full of emotions, anticipating

one that completes it. Then filling in
shades of light, each stroke and smear
a measure of luck for the one being

created. The subject sitting patiently on cue
as cells slough away unending death.
Contemplation heeds uncertainty, a tightrope

to walk from beginning to end.
Who is able to place themselves as permanently
as an artist's sketch? Every bit of countenance

interviewed, seen from outside in.
A snippet of Earth's time recorded
in utter perfection, one of her offspring

not dying, but coming into being.

Writing in Wartime

It's not the war.
It's the dominoes.
The war is far away

but the dominoes lie close,
their patterns of rolling dice
falling flat for us to see

foretelling a set of futures
undetermined
yet black and white.

A perverted butterfly effect
circling the globe
making us breathe differently

either infusing us with obligation
and hope, or adding to
fetid exhalations of surrender

to an outdated, unhappy
animal instinct.

Conscious

Listen: a raptor's call
from the trees. It bristles
the blood—gargled coo
down the spine.

In my dreams I have murdered
then buried the body parts.
I awaken smelling blood
as I blow my nose.

It's everywhere: our past.
Somewhere, some one of us—family—
has done this. We carry the memory
in our eyes, unleash instinct

under government orders. *I know*
I have murdered says the dream.
I know it's true. Where has my blood
roamed? Sardinia? Mongolia? Lebanon?

I smell the past about me, hanging
in the trees, dug under my garden.
Body parts are buried there. I see them
by my ancestors' eyes.

What one of us has done
will find us, one by one.

The Day the Bombs Fell

Men hid in the mountain park
dressed in white, as the white hare,
wolf, and perusing bear looked up
and twigs fell unevenly into snow.

Streams engendered jewels; fountains borne
of Rome lost nothing of their leonine
faces, spouting now for another
two thousand years.

Sun hit hard in the valleys, already suffering
reflections of far-off snow.
Cats perched defiantly in the breeze
counting their seconds of freedom.

Then the bombs fell, ripe watermelons
painting the earth red. Afterwards
the smoke gave up; dark winter clouds
pushed over the ridge, and snow
fell again on the burning towns

while soldiers in the mountainous woods
mistook the sound of thunder
for pealing bells, and saw each other as painted ghosts
too lost among the white winter animals
to know the world below.

The 9/11 Memorial

We stand at the edge, unable to pass
the walls of water and deep pool, its voided center
where all falls to God knows where

leaving us befuddled, anxious
that we find no direction.
Anonymous names resurface

in polished granite, yet we'll never know them.
This enormity has a double,
each its pool of unending despair.

How did this happen? What have we done?
Answers lie consumed by the echoless
water, its movement from what we know

to what pulls us down, relentless
as we keep an eye on it.

Congressional Cemetery

Herbert Hoover and his lover
lying four stones away.
John Philip Sousa muffled.

Well-heeled prostitutes
held down by stony angels.
Benches marking angles

to announce deaths to come.
A monument to gay pride
and military hypocrisy.

Bees buzzing their way
to volunteer gardens.
Chinese elms exhibiting

their mottled bark.
Our steps do little
to tamp down the soil.

Each footprint echoes
in common dirt.
Achievements wash away

as one grave equals the next
their contents neither raised nor diminished
by modified markers.

Gertrude Stein

Gertrude Stein said it's sad
that once you get older
you stop listening.

For those who were once captivated
by the timbre of a voice
by the thrill of not knowing

the thoughts it engendered
or the stillness between words
that grew into sweet confusion

that challenged every fiber
of past convictions, that kept you
up at night and tormented

your dreams so that you awoke
a new person, armed to start
a new day as someone

you never knew. Remember
those days.

The Land of Peace

Come to the land of peace.
Leave your hammer and nails behind.
Do not run. Do not call your mother

or children. Leave the woods,
those rock hideaways. Stand tall
and proud as bombs fall

around you. Come.
Answer the calling. Become one
with the open sky, the air

that has held the breath
of many others. Come
as you are; forget your dreams

and idle past. Walk softly
to make no disturbance.
Let your heart rise

and be your guide.
In the land of peace you will find
a child who has no words

who sits alone, waiting
to share a future.

A Secular *Our Father*

Our mentor who dwells in the spirit
let us not forget you.
We strive for a perfect society
but remember it comes only in days.

Remind us to honor our birthplace
that provides food, and direct us away from guilt
that comes from mistakes we make
as we'll know not to hold grudges.

Let us keep a sense of balance
between pleasure and responsibility.
Let us never lose faith
that we can only succeed together.

For we will find paradise, courage, and light
if we keep this pact with wisdom.

A Secular *Hail Mary*

Honor to women, poised and resilient,
as wise as men.

You who have given birth to every leader
shine in our memory.

Mother of all, remind us
that our shortcomings don't conquer hope
that we will find peace at death.

Blue

Blue bending over us, ants
crawling over the globe.
Our history living up there,

a constant reflection.
Look up and see
its gentle arc, its clouds

pinched at the edges,
their delicate suspension
after so many millennia.

Its silence rings louder than church bells.
Its light illuminates our every move.
Lie down and let it wash over you.

Surrender your folly, your central drama
for something that needs no direction,
no plan or vindication. It will find you

like an elusive benefactor, mother
with her arc of grace.

II.
PORTRAITS

When Your Spouse Speaks in Clichés

Remember that every word had
a beginning, coming from the mouth
of one who uttered amazement.

Remember that the impulse to gather emotion
pre-empts the ability to speak
that the seed of thought lies buried

in generations. Who are you to lambast
another's endeavor? Take a shovel
to your grief, find there the remains

of the first words you heard.
Likely you will uncover sentiments
that outlast dialects.

In the primordial sand is written *I love you.*
There is no other way to say it.

Switching Glasses

Mine are new, triple-focus
lenses, requiring some getting used to.

Hers haven't changed since her fourth-grade
eye examination, a lifetime

of fumbling in the dark, zeroing in
on my lips, cleaning contacts.

So now, after fifteen years, we switch
glasses. *You look cute in mine,* she says.

To me all is equally blurry.
Wo! She pulls back. *These make me*

dizzy. We look around—profiles
of curious chickens—then give

each other back. Comfort
lies in our individual worlds

and the infinite getting-to-know
from our views of finite selves.

That Day

I only knew what had been
offered me—in every direction
I saw moving planes of sunlight

among the blackened buildings
the smoke exhaust from mills
my intention to outline my view

and fill in the empty spaces.
She saw differently, more comfortable
in how she arranged life. And yet

I undid her focus.
I became more oblivious,
open to the cracks she pierced

through my wall of perception.
I had been interrupted.
Never again would I see art lessons

as a means of imprisoning what I hoped
to see. I began to notice new worlds
at every turn, one echoing

her voice, another her demeanor.
Everything I once disowned.

Love Prayer

I pray that love continue
to be blind, that annoyances
return to their vanishing act

that I see them not as shortcomings
other than my own, my vision
obscured by a useless march

toward perfection, that time
has only wrinkled us against a sea
of material clutter. That in the end

we will forget those in-between days
and come face to face
with each other, regard the fortress

we have built, and be relieved
that it is washed away.

The Things We Bought

The things we bought
now lie comfortably on their shelves
dusted by our presence.

The hillside drive seems
not as steep, the winter trees
lacing the night sky to appear

as we awaken. The chatter of red squirrels
subsides in January, a new year's weather
undecided. I pick up a white rock

of marble or quartz. It foretells our story,
the years that must pass in a ghosted house,
the sea on our doorstep, ready to carry us

to a final destination.

Sleep Doctor

Imagine a place, he said,
of utter calm; you were at peace
and nothing could interrupt it.

I saw a room with a bed
of honey-colored backboard spokes.
A Persian rug of subtle greens

and browns. My grandmother's old dresser
in the corner. A side table, box-shaped,
with a sticking door. Outside, a blazing maple

throwing color through daybreak windows.
Then a hissing radiator, snow falling
behind lace curtains. And you,

nestled in my arms after making love,
your skin as soft as forgiveness
in the face of uncertainty.

Our cat turning the door knob
before making his way to our bed
where he huddles at our feet

until dawn. Our two toddlers safe
in the next room, their door open,
as they grow their own dreams.

Now, he said, keep that
in your mind. Don't let anything
intrude. Come back again, and

you will fall asleep. If it worked before
it will work forever. Strange though
that you choose not to remember

a holiday beach, like everyone else.
That yours records a life
you never wanted to leave.

One Willow

One willow spilling its first shades
of green, everything else merely winking
as I speed by, forgetful, oblivious

to a warmth that grows from nothing.
A friend who calls to tell me
of his family's decline, mine

tucked away in the woods
where cold lingers enough
to fill me with regret.

I have not yet mastered
the school of abandonment.
It follows me through this green world

though I see only grays and brown
expecting the cold to go on
until I cannot remember

the words my ancestors spoke.
How they caress, flutter, persist.

A Name

In place of wondering what
other gifts, whose nose I have,
what color hair, the mannerisms they swore

were my father's. In place of oatmeal,
soft pajamas, candy on St. Nick's day.
In place of the free rein I had

in the back seat of our Chevy Bel Air.
Or the stock pot, half my size,
they allowed me to take to Nana's

so I could bang its lid all day.
In place of whatever they thought
I might become, or what they allowed

or denied me. In place of my father's absence
after he died, or my mother's fear
that she could not do it alone—

They gave me a name, a gift
so that I would always be located
within myself. So that they could rest

and let my name provide a course
unimaginable to them; so that
every time it was mentioned

I would grow more resilient,
more certain, more of everything
they never gave me.

Enough.

Just Before My Father Died

Before they took the dividing wall down
the dining room was a living room
tight as it was, even more crowded

with a Christmas tree tucked in the corner
its aluminum tinsel strands gently swaying
from furnace forced air.

All night the room warmed, combatting
the draft of old windows and storms
making their way to our home.

I don't remember them meeting me
at the stairs, just the glow of the room
and the shock of this other world

that had appeared as I slept. The presents
were a thrill, but as I grew older
and wondered if I really believed

what was happening, it all
came down to this: the invisible man
in the red suit was gone.

What remained was a Christmas
when love took over the room
and held me in its arms

something I could not have imagined
no matter how many props they put up,
none of them as needed.

On Reading the Death Certificate

On reading the death certificate
of my father, aged 29, my brother said
What do you make of the interval

between onset and death?
What do I make of the tiny cells
that stood ready to multiply

in the deepest part of his brain?
How long did they wait there?
In the interval between onset and death

he hopped the rooftops of a Pittsburgh
neighborhood with his cousin Ralph.
In the interval between onset and death

he sat diligently in a high school
political theory class, wondering what part of him
reared by Italian immigrants

might allow him to speak. In the interval
he sat with our mother in the booth
of the drug store soda fountain.

In the interval they found each other's bodies
on their wedding night, amazed.
In the interval he drove over snowy roads

to pick up our grandmother from the 54C
streetcar, a boxful of pizzelles in her hand.
He measured out pills, elixirs, and ointments

in a profession that allowed him to find order
in a senseless world. In the interval
he forgot who he was, his senses slowly dulled

as he lay breathing in a hospital bed
surrounded by blinding lights, remembering
reels of home movies of us he'd shot

wondering what might have been real.

Waiting Patiently in My Grandfather's Sardinia

Unsure of my Italian, the names
of surrounding trees, or which animal
rings a solitary bell in the distance

I sit on the old terrace, a pair of yellow wings
fluttering in and out of view.
They hover close then disappear

unsure of their welcome. The hills reverberate
my Pittsburgh childhood, footholds
of mills that turned immigrant hands

into steel. Another child learns
the ways of sheep. I see him
through a curtain of time. It envelops me

and returns a hundred years.
The butterfly continues, sneaking glimpses
from all angles, wondering whether

I can, or will, accept it.
Whether it too can peel back the curtain
or make sense of intervening decades.

A grandson never known in life
has returned to a life that knew pain
to forget. Hesitation hangs

on both sides, an inability to forge
that bridge, though pulses of yellow light
burn through. It only takes

the cool flutter of wings, a pair of eyes,
a memory that bears itself
even if it goes unnoticed.

The Boy at the Window

I see my grandfather as a little boy
looking out his bedroom window
into the dark, his brothers
and twin sister asleep.

He wears a worried expression
unaware of where it leads—
beyond the soft outline of Sardinian hills
to the streets of a sooty Pittsburgh.

He sits ensconced in visions
that trouble and thrill dark eyes.
He will have a family, a boy
who will outlive him. What views

will he see from foreign windows?
Why does the past mingle with a future?
A little boy in Sardinia, a place
his mother calls home, who serves him

honeyed bread every morning after the darkness
has left. Does air feel the same
everywhere? It comes in cool
from the window, and he allows it.

This is his secret time, a time
of no mother and father,
a time he can't share
because it reaches inside him

and uncoils, a time he will remember
while lying on his deathbed
lapsing into his boyhood tongue
that nobody understands.

Before lying down to sleep
he takes a hard look out the window.
He accepts the dark, finds beauty
and adventure there, even as

it brings a chill that no mother
will ever warm away.

I Went to Visit My Mother's Grave

I went to visit my mother's grave
in blindness. I placed a rose
on the stone, said my prayers

and walked away. The wind rose,
lifting the flower so it twirled
in the rain-soaked air, then landed

behind her name. The stem grew roots.
Tiny leaves sprouted along its length.
I didn't come back for many years.

The stem became a flowering bush,
its sprawling canes trembling.
One minute storm, the next

an August idyll. Inside each flower
grew a memory, a sculpture
of time as delicate

as its protection. When others passed by
they saw not the rose bush
but hands that brushed my hair

gentle smiles of approval
words that were never spoken
grown into blind love.

A Flock of Birds

Passing, keeping to their core, originating
over other lives, holding those stories
in air. Birds flying only

in one direction, seeing only sky, not
the gray silence. To stop would mean
falling to their deaths, the burial ground

of those who have looked up. In one sweeping gesture
they wrap up all that has happened,
steady in their rhythm, spirits

buoyed by beating wings. We fly with them
and don’t look back, passing over earthly grays,
closing our eyes to see color

and taste the lingering breath
of those who lie below.

Sling

They've taken my right arm
and set it into a sling.
Six weeks or so, enough to let

my new shoulder lodge
into place. It's not so bad
being one-handed. Time goes

more slowly. I approach every task
with great care, buttoning my shirt
and scrambling my eggs as if

for the first time.
But in the back of my mind
is that photo of Aunt Connie

at my sister's five-year birthday—
her face half-smiling, left arm
laid into a cloth tied up

to her neck, my grandmother
standing close, as if to catch her
in the next moment. Hobbling

into our backyard, she sat herself
into a swing, right hand grasping
the rope, right foot pressed into the grass

to rock herself gently.
A second stroke took her
before my third year, but I still see

her beautiful dark eyes
as she handed me a gift too
that day, and I fell in love

for the first time.

Memories Don’t Have Feet

Memories don’t have feet.
They move by willpower
shapeshifting from blank

to translucent, freeze frames
that mottle the air
with their enticing perfumes

leading us to believe
they are one with us.
As they reappear

we try to pin them down.
They flicker like a grandmother’s
hands tied up in yarn,

her crochet needle bouncing up and down
as she weaves that blue-and-white blanket
I’ve kept for fifty years.

Our Secret

Looking up in the center of darkness,
the world asleep, I stood
in the alleyway beside our door
hesitant for a moment, a full Moon

looking down, her circle of light
washing over me, where I pondered
the birth of my daughter.

We stayed there in eternity,
the Moon and I, our secret gone
as I opened the door.

Thirty-two years later I revel with others
at her wedding celebration, whites and golds
lighting the way, unaware that time
is passing. We have too much to forget.

I leave as others hang on.
I’ve played my part, dancing feet
hurting, throat relieved post-speech.
Finding my way in the dark, I look up.

My Moon, two days past full,
lights me again in its cycle,
warms my shoulders, tells me it’s okay
to let her go, dries tears before they fall.

Back in Place

I cut the dried stalks
of past years, the winters
I've held in my heart.

The roots of crabgrass give
and I must pat the bulbs
back into place.

Already the sun is breaking
warming these plots back to life.
The fountain I once constructed

still holds water, a dead dragonfly,
a pump that bubbles in confusion.
My little girl comes to plant whole peppers

one at a time. *Will these grow?*
she says. *I think so,* I reply.
None of this has happened.

I awaken to remember
that in those days I planted hope
that revisits me in time.

Miscarriage

I heard a woman sing
on the radio today. She mentioned
her father in clear, resonant notes

that carried me away.
I have two kids; neither
likes to sing. I love them very much.

But that one who left us
at the end of winter—
What voice never spoke

or sang? Sometimes I hear
notes in the air, calling me back
to uncertain times, situations

that never resolved, or others
that pinned me in place.
Yet I pretend to go on

living in the present as if
those past gifts must remain
unopened. I love my children

even the one who sings to me
in my sleep, whose face
I will never recognize

but for a slight movement
in the air, of notes that echo
an unbroken song.

The Tending Tree

I planted a tree in memory of someone
who opened a door for me, who let me lie
next to her soft collie, to feel

her cool linoleum floor in summer heat
bang her pots and pans as a toddler
taste the ice cream her husband made.

I planted a tree somewhere,
I don't know where, that may grow
in a distant family's yard, guard

the edge of a wood, shade tender weeds
or harbor insects, mammals, and birds—
like the parakeet laid into a shoebox

we buried beneath a cherry tree
in an untended part of her yard.
The funeral we held, the way

she kept me from falling apart, knowing
that my love would be tended there
by a tree.

Time Travel

I step out
as I'm obliged.

My two-year-old toddler
rides my back, holds my hand

as we cross the street.
Uncle Norman rides in my veins,

noting the red geraniums
and magenta potted profusion

that cascades to the ground
in my mother's front yard.

She is here too, her innocence
marking every turn I take

in New York's hub of blatant
sophistication. I count my homes—

those of my scattered youth
the sanctuary of our young family

the intermittent rest stops
of apartments and vacations.

They all trail me,
backdrops and foregrounds,

phantoms of color
redistributing my moods

in spite of the flying present.
There's only so much we can

handle, a wild mix of images
our eyes must accept

as they repeat in lonely intervals
like dreamcatchers that follow us

from one waking moment to the next.

III.
PAUSE

Stranded

Stranded in Old Greenwich, Connecticut
in a room without windows.

Having tossed ten holiday catalogues, unread,
into the trash.

Staring down vintage furniture
that once defined us, pictures on the walls

that have no clue where they are.
A flower my wife gave me the only

living thing I see, but even that will pass.
I've tried to corral the past

into my computer, yet it's dead
at the moment, so I rely only

on my brain's memory bytes.
The floor is cold; my feet need socks

though I'd rather walk barefoot through grass
and Whitman's every leaf of poem.

Those warm August nights we slept outside
with crickets and bats and raccoons

and shooting stars, how satisfied
we were to be blank slates,

how we never wished for the walls
of kitchens and living rooms.

How we loved our aching backs
and cold feet the next morning

in a yard that had made room
for all the living.

Galaxy Eyes

A lizard's eye on a billboard
Jurassic Park-like, staring at passers-by
leaving only an impression

of concentric circles in drivers' eyes
dimming light, star-studded, ending
in one dark slit. It's as if

the soul of the planet were watching
as its progeny roll by in self-appointed
haste, a hint of where we are

denied: this cloud of compacted dirt
revolving about one humdrum star
amid a swath of multicolored others

encircling the black core, one of many
similar galaxies that may have no one
to acknowledge them, though they stare at us daily

from the encircled patterns of colored light
in the eyes of individual creatures
each ending in the same dark center.

Pause

Aqua, indigo, blues
that come and go. Water
holding them in an arc

that reaches our sandy feet.
The sky colors too, clears
for composed clouds.

How many lives have we lived?
In one I run through mud
at the edge of a Pennsylvania creek,

the trees heavy, hazy, and still.
In another I peer through a window
to a hurricane gone berserk.

Now we are reborn in a faux
paradise, making us question
whether we've ever lived

as prisoners of an age,
our scars now tinted rose
lying under Caribbean sun

where they welcome us with eyes
that tell their own stories
in colors we will never know.

Under Water

The sea spills in from afar
filling our bay—its lost caverns
and glacial carvings—

with melted glass. We sit
on our steady float
nearly surrounded

knowing the water may rise and fall
even become white-capped,
as violent as any past.

We feel thunder under water
that reaches not only to Japan
but to pre-tectonic time.

It might rise up one day
and reclaim us all—progeny
who have drifted too far

thinking we could name
our age *Anthropocene,* as if
three-fourths of the globe

had no say.

High Tide

Clouds I hadn't noticed, full of rain
but never yielding, offering us
a long walk under gray canopy
until we reach the little lake, its gentle borders

rimming autumn grass, the ducks
curiously absent, turtles neglecting
their roam. My dog follows an old path
safe in its circle, the cool water still

and unassuming in its idyll.
We meet a friend and talk away
the day, other dogs casually approaching,
young couples spreading the lawn

with toddlers and towels. We part
in opposite ways, but the path I've taken
is now overgrown: the lake spilling out
in every direction, filling the grass, the path,

even the little bridge that formerly offered protection.
We turn around, unsure that we'll make it
before the lake consumes everything in silence,
taking cue from the weighty clouds,

both carrying out a master plan
that leaves little room for us.

The Great Escape

The ocean waves—crest and trough—
ambling through a physics amplitude
roar in soft echo
and refuse to be named.

I heard them once in childhood,
imagined whole fleets of adventure
and the cold depths of wonder
before I learned the chemistry

of water, the salinity of our bodies
and ancestry of sand. I heard the roundness
of our globe, the trade winds of history
etched into textbooks.

Now I've given up on learning
the hows and whys of everything.
The waves roll back, and I go
with them, back to a time

that was once mine, a music
of inception, not discovery;
a willingness to see, at last,
the beginning of everything.

Fossil Flowers

So, we’ve finally uncovered you
hiding in plain sight
for a hundred millennia.

Now we can photograph you
write poems about you
paint your portrait.

It’s no longer possible for you
to live in anonymity.
We now assume responsibility

for your looks, the way you
dandied yourself up
in a world of muted color

to say nothing of your long struggle
to become. It took fire
to preserve you, ashes

to make your bed.
But we will never know
the glory you felt

as you lifted your head one morning
and felt the sun, as you stood
proudly among others

who would greet you
with a windborne kiss
and together conquer

a sterile past.

Morning Sheds Light

Morning sheds light
on the dead, each still fern
and emerald leaf a phantom
of dusk, pinned in a place

of false hope, of all
that will not last. It's as if
Earth's heart beat once
its electricity holding

for this intimate portrait—
the tide still deciding where
it will go, animals awakened
but shocked into inaction.

A pulse gathers in defiance
breaking through this premonition.
The hours ascend, light turns to shade
and tiny footsteps dent the forest floor.

The Trees Lay Their Shadows

The trees lay shadows
in moonlight, over snow.

The deer and fox have passed.
A barred owl sits on dark branches.

The hardened life of oaks and pines
falls effortlessly to the ground.

They have all night to reach out,
celebrate this ghost

that flows over snow, synapses
that fire without sparks.

The shadows move
with the curving light

elongate, then shorten,
bask in conversation.

Who knows what they have unentangled
during this mystery of wholeness

allowing a mirrored life, absent
in the tangled light of summer.

I'm Out of Business

I'm out of business.
A lifetime of spare change
falls from my pockets.

No more errands to run.
My partners have gone extinct.
I can't even imagine

those timely transactions.
They were always invisible,
their riches illusory,

spent before accrued.
They have returned now
outside my window—

leaning trees death-defying
as their leaves cling
to an outdated season

and snow soon falls
to muffle every bud
safe in its future

a commerce neither sought
nor denied.

A New Autumn

I have been eating trees
with my eyes, ears, and nose.

Their colors soften
a bitter landscape

creating a welcome amnesia—
days when I gobbled them up

in paint, words, or dreams.
But trees remained outside

of me, petrified by my plan.
I killed them one by one.

Now I know their leaves
must shake, rattle, and fall

whether I note them or not.
Whether my dreams give them back

or I digest them into oblivion.

Storm

The deck looks wider as storm clouds
loom in the west. Empty flower urns
hold their ground; twigs break.
The tallest trees sway

and some will fall.
It will happen while we sleep.
But for now I stand behind a glass door
at room temperature, hands in pockets

knowing it never mattered how many times
I've swept that deck, or what flowers
I carefully placed in the urns.
The water beyond begins to churn.

Whitecaps overturn our tranquil
summer days. The newly planted native sod
crouches under dead leaves, its dainty stems
subject to the force that is coming.

For a moment I too am caught
in the thrill, knowing that uncertainty
is all we have, that everything rearranges
according to no one's whim

as I look forward to surveying destruction.

Louis Rakes the Hedges

Louis rakes the hedges clean
leaving me with tangled thoughts
as I watch from the window.

He works with one bandaged arm,
stooping carefully, digging out debris
and carrying it off like a box
full of puppies.

Yesterday I cleaned the hearth
and scattered rose petals over the remnant
ash. Their red lips circle in the white
and ignite flames of memory
where once charred logs stood.

This spring we see flowers developing
in all stages; that common freak, weather,
has torn us again, leaving the magnolia
two weeks behind, the hyacinths
double-stalked. I will wait

and let Louis comb the yard,
settling in the even parts
and picking up the pieces
of a stormy winter.

And I will wait for another cold day
when the rose petals have all dried
their scent blazing the dusty air
in the crackling flames of chance.

I Could Live There

A colonial perched
on a leafy hillside—its yard
a backslope of rhododendron
and weed, a bit of grass
here and there—

I could live there, I think
as the train rolls by.
Then I see a perfect wood
of evenly spaced pines
and long to lie on the warmed

fallen needles, their scent a relief
from housekeeping tedium.
I imagine other homes I've seen
on my journeys, how each embodies
another fantasy of mine

before they disappear into the next.
Now I live in an idyll
of woodland and sea, native plants
requiring little care, as rivulets
carve out their course, crows caw

and everyone who visits says
I could live here.

IV.
MEDITATIONS

What Do You Need for a History?

A memory that says *I was there*
even if you didn't want to be.
Another version of self
that flip-flopped between what you were
and weren't. A vague premonition

of a better future, even if
you didn't believe it.
Rings of fire you jumped through
the burns coming later
dried up into scars.

A checklist that defined everyone
but you. Following a way
that offered spectacular views
of foreign lands, climates
there to nurture unknowns.

And those times you strayed
holding your heart in calloused hands—
blood trailing—you were there
but once, and no one noticed
when you were gone.

Quitter

Quit your job.
Lose everything.
Strike up a conversation

with the dry cleaner.
Find a face—no matter
the expression. Shed

your skin, the years
it carries. Take a walk
to a city you've never seen

or the countryside full
of fallen leaves. Hear them
crunch underfoot. Watch

for hints of life—
the curling snake
or foraging bobolink.

Breathe in the air
of centuries, the gift
of regeneration.

Forget that you ever
were, then relish
your rebirth.

Let misfortunes evaporate
into stars, distant reminders
of those you loved.

On this day
nothing will matter
but what you see.

Feel your heart as it lifts
to dizzying heights.
Let your feet kiss the earth

one more time
before you leave.

I Keep Being Reborn

I keep being reborn
on a Monday afternoon in Connecticut
having passed through Maine and Massachusetts

the rain come and gone
as we head for an inn we had known
twenty-five years ago.

My hands, firmly attached to the wheel,
direct us through roads unknown
those so close to that life of child-rearing

and making ends meet. I shudder
to remember the streets of my youth,
unsettled to feel that my eyes

still see a countryside awakening
as my stomach aches to be filled
my limbs as nimble

as a ten-year-old's riding a bike
or steadying my daughter as she presses
her first pedal. I should be gone by now

I think, but every time I blink
I am reborn. No need for a new religion
or heart transplant. This journey

will never come to an end
as long as I catch my breath
on the next turn.

That Moment

The moment I lost my childhood
I sat in an unfamiliar room
listening to a transistor radio.

I had slept there
hundreds of times, awakened
to the same dim days.

Now it was different. Something
tied me down, taut as a springboard
that would release me.

But I didn't know when.
I waited. I left my life
and entered the radio's, its turquoise case

brighter than the sky, playing songs
that would burn all the way
to my sixties, when I would finally feel

no strings attached.

At Ten Years Old

At ten years old I liked cars.
At thirteen, girls.

At sixteen, my studies.
At twenty-one, writing.

At twenty-five, melancholy.
At twenty-eight, panic.

By thirty, my wife.
And thirty-five, two kids.

At forty, I started to like myself.
At forty-eight, colors again.

At fifty, confidence.
At fifty-five, realization.

At sixty, I didn't give a shit.
At sixty-three, I'm letting you know.

I Did

Yes we did.
We peed on Cadillac door handles.

Don't ask me why.
I'll tell you why—

None of us had Cadillacs
and we didn't know anyone

who owned a Cadillac.
So we peed on them to let them know

we were displeased. Owners
would grab their handles

and feel the stickiness
of our youth, maybe wonder

why they had bought a Cadillac
while driving home

to that mythical place
where everyone owned Cadillacs.

The News

As a hormone-driven adolescent
I took in the news—not only
the cascade of events around me

but around the globe, the wars,
the crime, the yin-yang
of republicans and democrats.

I had solid opinions then.
It all seemed so clear.
I campaigned in a mock election

my convictions outweighing uncertainties
about where I was headed. The news
finally consumed me, and I was left

with one direction, no forks in my road.
So I gave up on current events.
Life was more interesting.

Fifty years on I find I cannot escape
a pandemic, the erosion of our rights,
ecocide, a new war

that might spell the end of us.
I've resisted being a consumer.
I don't want to be eaten again

by the news. I'd rather find the future
in a woodland plant, a life drama
as told by a new acquaintance,

my dog's sideward glance when I speak to her.

In These Times

I come back to a room
sided with high windows
looking out to a forest

of tall pine, deciduous trees
cloaked in bud. I return
as a grandfather, a new bit of me

I never imagined. The room
stills beyond years, those times
we sat in a cabin with a sliding door

that led to a new world.
This house is perfect.
Yet we awaken to water leaks

and clogged drains. I fear
the morning news, a flipped coin
to my bliss. I know it teeters

like never before, images of war
and the life of my grandchild
unbearably uncertain.

It's all in my head, I know,
even as I make plans to teach him
gardening, to draw, to paint

his own world, no matter
what curtains may be pulled away.

Tabula Rasa

Three books lie unopened.
My wife lies absently on the couch
gone to a digital novel world.

A fire heaves in its designated hearth.
I am in and out of it
in and out of my thoughts

as my body grows older.
Lacking the courage to write them down
I flounder in semi-sleep

remembering the title of a news article
proclaiming the latest discovery: that
in our universe, present and future occur

simultaneously. I think about
the poems I've written, love letters,
fiction. It all comes back

yet future plans delete them
from a list of accomplishments.
There is too much death on the horizon,

a triumphant *tabula rasa*
that I will remember
where nothing is written.

Old Shirts

My beloved T-shirts, worn ragged,
washed to the color of dust, yet
imprinted with my scent

carry everything I've witnessed—
their first days of my rejuvenation,
trial period of comfort, final stretch

of willful obscurity—
as I met with triumph and despair
watching the orioles return,

my mother die, the sunlight of seawater,
my daughter admitted to rehab.
In the end I retire them

to the taboret of my painting studio
where, one by one, I use them to collect
excessive brushstrokes, unplanned arrays

of cadmium color, as I create new worlds
on a blank canvas, and those second skins
provide new comfort, their abandoned lives

awakened to new purpose.

Today I Write, Not Paint

I lay strokes of rich vermillion
verb, burnt sienna noun, a clandestine
highlight of adjectival white.

A thousand hues were not
enough for what I'd had in mind.
Seeing is deception, never the final

say. Feel-good umber is no replacement
for the palimpsest of feeling
that flickers from A to Z.

On my palette, last month's colors
slowly solidify, static choices
I may amend. How many paintings

have been made after poems?

I Am a Rock Band

Or no. I've never been in a rock band.
Today's poets, a friend once called them.
Who reads poets otherwise?

I wanted to be the lead, the guy
who wrote the songs, bared his heart on stage,
never combed his hair. But I didn't.

I wanted to bang out rhythms on the drums.
In fact I do that all day long with my fingers
on tables and chairs. But the novelty wears off.

Basslines have always thrilled me, but so does
the phrase or two that never leaves my head
until their vibrations reach paper.

What about the backups who provide
thrilling harmonies or counterpoint?
Without them a song is barren. But now I see—

They are the articles, conjunctions, and pronouns
that dress the lead. A guitar riff
or sullen organ note is all a poem needs

to give a lasting impression. And oh, the voice
that lingers in the reader, uniquely heard
a personality composed of lead thought

of rhythm and pulse and pause
before opening up again to silence:
a raucous rock band's echo composed.

Stepping Out

Stepping out into the Maine light
following a night of ache and darkness
I find the glinting foil of chipped water

and hesitate to believe I am not
imprisoned by a troubled past, life
borne only of tragic consequence

never as I am now.
This day has broken free
from my head; it has rested there

for decades, a song whose lyrics
were unintelligible, waiting for me
to place them within a broken

melody. I sing now newly
intact the notes that had been hidden.
It is enough to let them play

and not think to write them down.

Waiting for a Poem to Arrive

Waiting for a poem to arrive
the leaves swirl outside.
A late-spring snow becomes

another past, mingling with
those I want to re-imagine
those that gave me a lifetime

that begs validation, even forgiveness
though I had nothing to do with it.
How many days must pass

before I can garden again?
Before I lose this stalemate
of judgement, of ordering a persistent

disorder? Let the sun rain down
the wind kick up its heartfelt chaos
and the bay's waves resettle

into their silent complacency.
I will wait for the arrival
of another stately chapter

in the book of my undoing.

Rolling

The 4:39, always on time
and never crowded, passengers
coming and going from trashy
New Haven tracks to elegant Darien

where handsome men and women unzipper
their world to step into a red and white
carriage on wheels. I doze, read,
but mostly pay my respects

to a film I can't help watching—
red-tailed hawks roosting beside I-95,
skeletal warehouses, a lotful of Jaguars,
Black boy carefully shoveling snow.

Coastal marshlands *sans* human footprint,
incomprehensible graffiti, posters calling us
all to New York, Jamaican women who get off
at Bridgeport—a panoply of impressions

that eat away at mine, call me
to an order I'm not sure I want.
For I've stored my own images, moment by moment,
in a vault of freeze-frames that resist rolling by.

From the Corner of My Eye

From the corner of my eye
I see the Earth as it is:
suspended in darkness
the faint outlines of her continents,
quiet oceans. She heaves in circles

but I stay only with the night
a flicker of what I remember
back to what I see.
I don't know whose eyes
I've been granted: mine

or those of all who once spotted
the ghosted globe. It would be better
to awaken to misted waterfalls
and chattering birds, to enter
the morning fog, lick blood

from my wounds. But I am stuck
in this unhappy perspective
of what came before and after.
The stars unreachable. Solar systems
spinning in each of my cells.

I'd Forgotten

I'd forgotten.
In intervening years my kids
had grown; those I'd taught

now have kids of their own.
We're all in the business of getting by,
forfeiting the rocky past

in favor of a cutting-edge present.
Here comes a busload of tech-school students
interrupting my plans for a road-trip lunch

delaying my order, clogging the pick-up counter
eyes darting from pain to insecurity
and that adolescent SOS that begs forgiveness

while asking direction. The years peel back
as I wait. A teacher apologizes
on their behalf, but I have little more to say

than *It's okay.* I rethink all those Ivy conversations
that have been suffocating the boy in me
and stand patiently, surrounded

by a beautiful chaos of upwardly reaching souls
the kind that teach us reverence
for their delicate balance.

First the Berlin Wall

First the Berlin Wall fell.
Then two of my friends died.
My mother got a liver transplant.

Fatherless as child, I sired a daughter
and a son. I made it up
as I went along, my wife caressing

all doubt from me. The seeds of my childhood
sprung up anew. My ancestors' lives
made sense, their secrets

become second nature. But nature
I could no longer take for granted.
She pelted me with uncertainty

shifting her responsibility
to me. My gardens no longer followed
the seasons. They waited to see

what I might do. Now I am
at the crossroads, frenetic
to cast my vote. Do I live

in the shadow of my upbringing?
Or hold out an olive branch to chance
and follow the fearless *sempervirens?*

The Runway

A spot of light grows
but stays distant.
I spy it from my window

in an airtight hotel
where they've installed
a blackout curtain

to keep noise and light
at bay. The airliners land
along a runway that lends

perspective, a vanishing point
of glowing light I cannot
keep from seeing.

How long will it hover
above the horizon, speeding
in a straight line

that never comes closer?
If I turn away
will it disappear

or find its way
in its own time, leaving me
protected in the dark?

About the Author

Mark Saba, a native of Pittsburgh, is the author of poetry collections *Flowers in the Dark* (Kelsay Books, 2023), *Calling the Names,* and *Painting a Disappearing Canvas*. He also writes fiction, including *The Shoemaker, Two Novellas: A Luke of All Ages/Fire and Ice* and *Ghost Tracks: Stories of Pittsburgh Past*. His stories, poems, and creative nonfiction have appeared widely in literary journals across the United States and abroad.

He worked for 33 years at Yale University as an illustrator and graphic designer. Now he spends his time writing and painting at his new home in Maine with his wife, savoring visits from their grandchildren.

www.ingramcontent.com/pod-product-compliance
Lightning Source LLC
LaVergne TN
LVHW010627100826
845148LV00014B/3137

* 9 7 9 8 9 0 1 4 6 8 1 2 8 *